Original title:
Life: Not a Puzzle, Just a Mess

Copyright © 2025 Creative Arts Management OÜ
All rights reserved.

Author: Sophia Kingsley
ISBN HARDBACK: 978-1-80566-101-6
ISBN PAPERBACK: 978-1-80566-396-6

Scribbles of Uncertainty

In the chaos, I trip and fall,
Chasing dreams that bounce off walls.
Coffee spills and socks don't match,
Who knew luck would make a catch?

Nothing's ever quite on track,
Maps are crumpled, did I miss a snack?
Each detour brings a new surprise,
Like a clown balancing on pies.

Chance Encounters in a Tidal Wave

Riding waves on a wobbly board,
I find camaraderie with a flaming sword.
Laughter erupts, we take the plunge,
What's more thrilling than the random lunge?

A seagull steals my last fry,
While a crab scuttles, oh my, oh my!
Saltwater kisses under a blue sky,
Who knew chaos could soarly fly?

Harmony in the Havoc

In a whirlwind dance, we sway and spin,
Tripping over shoes that just won't win.
Joyful shouts and giggles loud,
Making peace in a crowded crowd.

Spilled confetti joins the fray,
Silly hats here to stay.
Finding rhythm in the mess,
Who knew chaos could impress?

Poetry Beneath the Piled Debris

Underneath this mountain high,
Lies a treasure, oh me, oh my!
Old takeout boxes, an empty jar,
Hiding wonders, just a tad bizarre.

A lost sock whispers sweet tales,
Of adventures through thrifting gales.
In the clutter, joy's parade,
Messy moments never fade.

Embracing the Unruly

My socks are dancing, what a sight,
One's in the fridge, it's feeling light.
The dishes conspire, they pile and pile,
Yet somehow we manage to smile.

Spilled cereal looks like modern art,
Each day's a giggle, a brand new start.
Forgotten keys sing a jingle tune,
We'll find them someday, maybe in June.

Journey Through the Jumble

Maps are scattered, lost with the mail,
Yet we sail on snacks and the occasional trail.
Left turns and right turns all turn to fun,
Who needs a plan when you've got the sun?

Bumps on the road bounce us in cheer,
Laughter echoes, we've no time for fear.
Bring on the chaos, let's take a ride,
The driver's a cat, but we'll be fine!

The Poetry of Imperfection

A crooked picture on top of a heap,
It's more character than we will keep.
Each wiggle and wobble tells a bold tale,
Of socks and of spoons that can't seem to bail.

Problems like puzzles, such a tall stack,
But give them a poke, they might just crack.
With smiles as our glue, we mend the fray,
Imperfectly perfect, we find our way.

Celestial Clutter

Stars in the kitchen, a comet in bread,
Aliens abducted the last thread.
Planets collide, and cups overflow,
It's a stellar mess, but look how they glow!

Galaxies twinkle from under the bed,
With nonsense and stories alive in our head.
Astronauts laughing in mismatched shoes,
In this cosmic chaos, we cheerfully cruise.

Unchained Whimsy

In the kitchen, pots collide,
A dance of spatulas on the ride.
Eggs may splatter, pancakes burn,
Yet laughter echoes, and we learn.

Socks that wander, shoes that stray,
Every morning's a new ballet.
Coffee spills like morning cheer,
As chaos plays, we persevere.

The Fragments We Carry

With buttons missing, shirts untucked,
We wander forth, a bit unplucked.
Lost keys jingle, wallets hide,
Yet through the mess, we laugh and glide.

Stories written on our sleeves,
In mismatched shoes, we deceive.
Left turns taken, right paths missed,
In each sweet blunder, joy persists.

Jigsaw of the Unseen

Pieces scattered, colors wrong,
Yet somehow, we hum along.
A hairpin journey in the sun,
With tangled threads, we still have fun.

Who needs straight lines in the end?
We twist and turn, around we bend.
A puzzle? Nah, it's just a show,
With silly hats, we steal the glow.

Vignettes of the Unscripted

Impromptu dances in the rain,
With mismatched steps that quite entertain.
Lullabies sung off-key and loud,
In the midst of chaos, we're still proud.

Spaghetti thrown upon the wall,
A culinary grand free-for-all.
Echoes of laughter in the air,
In this mess, we find our flair.

Knotting Together the Disjointed

Socks are missing, shirts don't match,
A spoon found in the cat's new stash.
My keys took a stroll, don't know where,
Oh look, there's a sandwich in my hair!

Plans collide like cars in a race,
Tripping over shoes in my own space.
The dog's got a snack—no, it's my lunch!
We're always late, but hey, it's a hunch!

Mosaics of Memory and Mayhem

Fragments of days all jumbled tight,
Forgotten the stew, just the fridge's fright.
Did I wear this hat yesterday too?
Maybe that's why my cat's giving the boo.

Mix-up my calendar, it's quite the show,
A birthday bash for someone I don't know.
But the cake looks good and free drinks abound,
I'll dance like nobody cares to be found!

The Joys of Unfinished Stories

Once upon a time—I forgot the rest,
A twist in the plot? Just a big ol' mess.
Characters wandering without any aim,
Just sitting around, playing a game.

A hero is lost, a villain just snorts,
They met in a café, but missed all the ports.
With coffee cups clinking, they laugh and they sigh,
Who needs a resolution? Let's just fly high!

Unscripted Refrains

They say life's a song with notes that won't fit,
But I don't need lyrics, just a good split.
Off-key and quirky, let's dance in the rain,
A splash here, a splash there, rhythm's insane!

No set choreography, just wiggle and sway,
Stumbling through moments in a colorful way.
With laughter as music, let the chaos arise,
Every fumble a treasure, in our own eyes!

Dancing in the Disarray

Twirling socks and missing keys,
Chasing cats and dodging bees.
Stumbling through the daily spree,
Who needs order? Let's just be!

Spaghetti spills and coffee stains,
A dance of chaos, no refrains.
We laugh and trip, ignore the pains,
In this mad waltz, joy remains.

The toaster pops, the cat's on top,
Eggs on the floor, let's dance, don't stop!
Who needs a plan? Just let it flop,
In this wild groove, we laugh and hop.

So here we are, a merry crew,
Messy hair and mismatched shoes.
Wave goodbye to the straight and true,
In this crazy jig, we're born anew.

When Order Disappears

The laundry pile starts to sway,
A sock escapes, it's on display.
The plates are stacked in disarray,
Come join the fun, just disobey!

Puzzles half done, pieces stray,
Maps upside down lead us astray.
Yogurt spills in bright array,
Who knew chaos could be this gay?

The calendar's a jumbled mess,
A birthday party in excess.
Join the chaos, don't suppress,
Laughter rises, we feel blessed.

So throw your rules into the sea,
Embrace the madness, dance with glee.
In this wild whirl, you'll see,
Order's boring, let it flea!

Beauty Amidst the Blunders

Cracked screens and tangled wires,
Burnt toast, oh how it inspires!
A splash of paint, accidental fires,
Beauty grows where chaos tires.

Dinner burned but spirits rise,
Laughter echoes, no disguise.
We paint our dreams in strange ties,
In every mess, a sweet surprise.

The garden's full of weeds and cheer,
Flowers bloom, despite the sneer.
Each little blunder we hold dear,
In this parade, we persevere.

So toast the spills, the quirky ways,
In the mayhem, joy always plays.
Embrace the flaws, let's sing our praise,
In every mistake, love displays!

Scattered Pieces of the Heart

Fuzzy notes and broken strings,
Socks that dance, oh what joy brings!
A puzzling mess of little things,
Heart's wild rhythm, chaos sings.

Coffee cups like Jenga towers,
Plant pots tipped in late-night hours.
Amongst the mayhem, joy empowers,
Laughter blooms like springtime flowers.

Gifts unwrapped, the paper flies,
Best laid plans become our guise.
Every stumble, every rise,
In this patchwork, love complies.

So gather shards, let them unite,
In every mishap, find delight.
Our scattered pieces shine so bright,
In this grand mix, wrong feels right.

Wandering Without a Map

I traipse through streets, oh what a sight,
With maps forgotten, I stumble and fight.
My coffee spills, my shoes are untied,
But laughter erupts as I take it in stride.

Each corner bewildered, a new path I find,
Waving at ducks, leaving reason behind.
If confusion had legs, I'd be its best friend,
In this wild game, there's no need to pretend.

Embracing the Unexpected Chaos

I woke up this morning, the sun in my eyes,
Socks mismatched, what a grand surprise!
Juggling my breakfast while tripping on chairs,
This glorious madness? It surely has flair.

A phone call comes in, I can't find my shoe,
Lost in the chaos, what else is new?
The dog is now barking, the cat's on the fridge,
I smile at the mess, standing proud on this ridge.

The Canvas of Crumpled Pages

My diary is scribbled, with thoughts that collide,
Pages turned brown from the chaos inside.
A masterpiece formed of spaghetti and glue,
Dear author of mayhem, I commend you it's true.

With sketches of dreams that dart and then flee,
All penned in a frenzy, reminding me,
Not every great novel starts with a plan,
Sometimes wild scribbles are the best as they stand.

Moments Lost in the Mayhem

I searched for my glasses, they're perched on my head,
A typical morning, fueled by dread.
The coffee's too strong, I've spilled half a cup,
Yet here I am laughing, not giving a hup.

The kids are a whirlwind, they race down the hall,
While I'm stuck in slow motion, I can't help but fall.
Memories dance twirling, amidst all the mess,
In this curious circus, I always feel blessed.

Dances in the Dust

Dust bunnies twirl in the air,
Not a worry, just a mad flair.
Chasing shadows under the sun,
Laughter echoes, we're all just one.

Socks mismatched, shoes untied,
With every step, our plans collide.
We skip and tumble, laugh a lot,
Embrace the chaos, it's our shot.

The cat joins in, a clumsy paw,
Bouncing off the wall with a flaw.
Our party's wild, no rules in sight,
Just joyful hearts and pure delight.

So let's not fret, just dance around,
In dusty rooms, fun can be found.
Forget the pieces, let it be,
In this great mess, we're truly free.

Embracing the Beautifully Bizarre

A cupcake wearing a silly hat,
Broccoli insists it's a cool cat.
The toaster sings while the clock just grins,
Welcome to where the madness begins.

Umbrellas float like boats on air,
Worms recite poetry, if you dare.
Rabbits juggle while squirrels mime,
In this odd world, we're out of time.

Dance with the weird and the stray,
Confetti rains on a bright, blue day.
We'll spin 'round and laugh at the scene,
In our wonderfully weird routine.

So raise a toast to thoughts bizarre,
Collect the moments, they're worth a star.
With every quirk, our hearts align,
In this strangeness, we truly shine.

Fragments of a Haphazard Journey

Maps are crumpled, coffee spills,
Each turn we take, a new set of thrills.
Traffic's halted, we sing off-key,
In this chaos, we're simply free.

Lost my wallet, found a shoe,
The route's unclear, but what's new?
Behind the wheel, who needs a plan?
We're zig-zagging, yes, that's our jam.

Cows on the road, a slow parade,
We honk and laugh, dreams don't fade.
Headlights flicker, a beacon bright,
Navigating through the wild night.

So here's to roads with unexpected bends,
To fumbled laughs and our wild friends.
Embrace the twists, hold on tight,
In this messy ride, we'll find delight.

Serenade of Spilled Ink

Ink spills out like a wild stream,
Words collide in a chaotic dream.
Papers dance on the cluttered floor,
Each stroke of chaos we can't ignore.

Scribbles laugh, some lines just sigh,
Characters leap, oh my, oh my!
A plot that twists like spaghetti night,
Let's stir the mess, it feels so right.

Comics burst in colors bright,
As characters wander, taking flight.
Each page a journey, odd and free,
A joyous mess, just wait and see!

So grab a pen, embrace the spill,
Let's not be proper, but dance with thrill.
In our spilled ink, we'll craft our tune,
With laughter shared beneath the moon.

Twists and Turns of Time

Around the corner, lost I go,
Chasing shadows, moving slow.
With each tick, the clocks all wink,
Who needs order? Let me think!

Coffee spills, the toast is burnt,
In every mess, a lesson learned.
A dance with chaos, oh what fun,
Life's a riddle, but who's the pun?

My shoes are mismatched, what a sight,
I stumble but it feels so right.
Embrace the fumbles, wear a grin,
Who cares if I don't fit in!

Lifes' a circus, watch me jive,
Popcorn flies, I'm still alive!
Let's twirl and twine through this array,
In the whirl, we find our way.

Relics of the Unpolished

Here's a crumb with a story, I swear,
Captured laughter hangs in the air.
Dusty memories, a grand parade,
Messy histories, never fade.

Stains on the carpet, oh what a tale,
Of joyful dinners, and a grand fail.
With mismatched plates and forks askew,
Each slip and slide, a part of you.

The garden grows wild, weeds in bloom,
With every flower, there's still room.
A brilliant mess, a glorious patch,
Who knew the world could so mismatch?

A treasure map of odd and ends,
With colorful chaos, the heart transcends.
So laugh it off, let's raise a toast,
To relics we cherish, we love the most!

Songs for the Soul's Messiness

In tangled notes, the music plays,
Hitting the wrong keys, in a daze.
What's a tune without a blip?
Sing loud and proud, let laughter slip!

A chorus of giggles, life out of sync,
Dance with oranges, let the apples think.
With a trumpet blast and a squeaky shoe,
We'll write a ballad, just me and you.

Chorus of chaos, echoing cheer,
Each missed beat draws me near.
Spin in circles, don't miss the cue,
In messiness, we'll break through!

Let's hum and whistle off-key delight,
Brighten the shadows, ignite the night.
Each note a splash of vibrant zest,
In this mad symphony, we are blessed.

Threads of Fate in Disarray

Spinning yarns that tangle tight,
Each colorful strand is a new delight.
Maps of chaos, stitched by chance,
Step on the thread and join the dance!

Frays in the fabric, colors collide,
Every great story took a wild ride.
Weaving tales, both silly and bold,
In a mess of threads, true dreams unfold.

A patchwork of giggles, every tear,
Creating a tapestry beyond compare.
Fate's humor shines in the loose ends,
Life's greatest art, my dear friends!

So grab a thread, let's tie a knot,
In this muddled creation, give it a shot.
We'll stitch our blunders into a charm,
With every loop, it's full of warm!

The Melodies of Mayhem

When socks revolt and shoes conspire,
All plans fly high, like kites on fire.
My toast does a dance, jams take their stance,
Each morning's chaos is a silly chance.

The cat's on the counter, what a sight!
I'm brewing my coffee, but it's not quite right.
Pancakes flip over, oh what a mess,
Yet laughter erupts, oh, I must confess.

The car won't start, it gives a good cry,
I wave to the bus, but it zooms on by.
Each journey's a riddle, each turn's a jest,
In this daily circus, I'm truly blessed.

So bring on the madness, I'll take it all in,
With giggles and chuckles, there's no room for sin.
For in this great mess, joy takes its form,
And through all the chaos, my heart keeps warm.

Harmony in the Haphazard

Juggling errands, I drop a few,
Forgot the milk, what else is new?
My planner's a riddle, a mad-cap play,
Yet somehow I dance through the fray each day.

A recipe calls for an extra pinch,
But my flour's a mountain, oh, what a clinch!
Burnt toast is waiting, it sends up a smoke,
But laughter erupts, I'm not even broke.

The dog stole my sandwich, oh what a thief,
He munches with glee, gets my grief!
Amidst all the mishaps, I'm finding the light,
In chaos and giggles, I'm taking my flight.

So let's toast to the madness, the slips and the falls,
To the quirky little moments that life calls.
For in all this confusion, I find my own muse,
With a wink and a grin, I just can't refuse.

Wandering Through the Wildness

A map without directions, oh what a ride,
I'm lost in the wild, but I take it in stride.
Trees whisper secrets, birds sing their song,
In the tangled paths, I feel I belong.

My phone's in a frenzy, it says I'm here,
But with no road in sight, I laugh without fear.
The compass is spinning, like a top gone mad,
Yet with every wrong turn, I just feel glad.

The bushes might nibble, the trail may confuse,
Each twist in the journey, I gladly peruse.
With every odd corner, new wonders unfurl,
In this splendid mess, I'm embraced by the swirl.

So here's to the wanderers, lost in a dream,
Where laughter and chaos dance in one gleam.
For in every wild turn, there's magic to find,
In the heart of the ruckus, we're all intertwined.

Life's Chaotic Canvas

With brushes a-flying, paint splatters bright,
A masterpiece waiting in every slight blight.
Colors collide in a joyous parade,
In this artistic mess, I'm happily swayed.

Oh! What's this? A splash of bright green,
A whirlwind of hues makes my canvas obscene!
But as I create with a grin ear to ear,
The beauty of chaos becomes oh-so-clear.

Stains on my shirt, a palette of dread,
Yet I giggle and laugh, while I dance instead.
With every wild stroke, a story unfolds,
In this glorious muddle, creativity holds.

So raise up your brushes, let's cheer to the art,
In the mess and the mayhem, we find the true heart.
For in every splatter, a miracle lies,
A chaotic canvas, where imagination flies.

Reflections in a Rippling Stream

Fish swim past, making ripples,
As I toss in bread crumbs and giggles.
The ducks just waddle, unaware,
Of the chaos lurking everywhere.

I see my face, all twisted and strange,
Is that a duck or just my range?
Flotsam floats, in a grand ballet,
Who knew weirdness could swim today?

The Palette of an Unfinished Painting

A canvas splattered with wild hues,
A splash of red, a hint of blues.
What's this? A cat? Or just a blob?
Art or disaster, take your prob!

Brushes tangled like spaghetti strands,
Dancing freely, without commands.
Each stroke, a little bit of flair,
Is there a method? Who would care?

Serendipity in the Storm

Rain pours down, a wild parade,
Umbrellas flip, it's a grand charade.
Lightning strikes, we jump and swirl,
We might just trip—oh what a whirl!

A puddle forms, a perfect dive,
Who knew chaos could make us thrive?
We splash and laugh, what a delight,
Embracing mess like it's alright.

The Patchwork of Everyday Wonders

Socks don't match, but hey, who's counting?
Cereal's for dinner, my joy's mounting.
The dog wears glasses, thinks he's wise,
As we dance around, to our own surprise.

Chores pile high, a mountain disproportionate,
Yet we navigate—call it our fortunate.
Each phone call drops, a comedy scene,
In this wacky show, we reign supreme!

The Colors of a Broken Map

A map that leads to nowhere but my feet,
With paths that twist, a tangled sheet.
Red leads to blue, then yellow to green,
A chaotic route, a funny scene.

Directions fail, the signs are wrong,
Yet I hum my tune, and carry on strong.
Every wrong turn, a brand new chance,
To waltz in circles, a silly dance.

Markers fade like a prank on my mind,
Lost in the colors, oh what did I find?
A compass spinning, like a topsy turvy,
Skillful in flops, I'm never too nervous.

So here I roam with laughter out loud,
In a vibrant mess, I'm blissfully proud.
Each wrong turn lifts my spirits anew,
A riot of colors, my joy's coming through.

Scribbles on a Blank Page

A canvas so wide, with splashes of ink,
Squiggles and doodles, I stop to think.
The lines may muddle, the shapes may sway,
But isn't that fun in a scribbly way?

Thoughts like confetti, they scatter and fly,
I try to be serious, but I just laugh and sigh.
With curves and loops, my words engage,
Each twist a giggle, on this blank page.

Plans I've made, drawn in crayon hues,
Smudged with my finger, I'm free to choose.
A funny little quirk, this mess I create,
In chaotic compositions, I find my fate.

Learning to smile at my jumbled art,
These scribbles of mine play the funniest part.
For in the chaos, I truly find glee,
A masterpiece made just to amuse me.

Torn Pages of Existence

A book that's well-read, pages dog-eared,
Torn from the ride, but I'm never veered.
Each rip a story, a laugh or a tear,
With ink-stained fingers, I could not care.

The plot keeps twisting like spaghetti bends,
Chapters of chaos that never end.
I fumble through life like I'm turned around,
Yet humor finds me in lost tales I've found.

Did I mention the dog ate chapter three?
Or that page ten was caught in a tree?
But hey, it's all good; I'm still in the game,
With each page turning, I'm never the same.

So here's to the tales with pieces undone,
Each messy scrap makes for brighter fun.
Finding delight in this wild, tangled text,
There's beauty in chaos - who'd have guessed next?

Mismatched Socks and Unruly Dreams

My socks are mismatched, a colorful sight,
One's polka-dotted, the other's bright white.
Just like my dreams that come in a rush,
Some quiet like whispers, others a hush.

I skip through the day with odd little pairs,
Laughing at life, pretending no cares.
Tangled ambitions, chaotically spun,
Each twist an adventure, a wacky run.

Tangled up thoughts, like laundry piled high,
Some threads hold laughter, some leave you awry.
Connecting odd tales like each sock on my feet,
In fashion's rebellion, I find my heartbeat.

So wear those mismatches with pride on your chest,
For ordinary's boring; it's chaos that's best.
With a wink to the world, I prance as I sing,
In this mismatched existence, I find my own zing!

Finding Light in the Shuffle

Woke up today, socks don't match,
Found my keys in the fridge, what a catch!
Coffee spills on my shirt, a fashion statement,
Stumbling through chaos, I hardly lament.

Chasing my cat, she's plotting a heist,
In a box of old junk, she thinks it's a feast.
Life's little hiccups, they come with a grin,
Like juggling eggs when you're aiming to win.

Bikes need fixing, my tire's gone flat,
But I laugh at the mess, just look at that!
Each twist and turn, a circus of sorts,
Clowns riding unicycles, absurd laughs and snorts.

So here's to the shuffle, the giggles it brings,
Embracing the chaos, as laughter still sings.
Shuffle off worries, give joy a big shove,
In this wild, funny dance, we find what we love.

Echoes of the Unraveled

I walked down the street, tripped on my shoes,
Fell on a dog who gave me the blues.
They say 'watch your step', but I just stare,
At the circus parade I never had a care.

A sandwich I packed, forgot it at home,
Hunger's a beast when you're out all alone.
I laughed at a pigeon, it stole my last fry,
This day's a fairground, oh my, oh my!

Lost in the crowd, the map's upside down,
Searched for a smile, but found a frown.
Yet in all the chaos, a rhythm I hear,
A jazzy connection, no need for fear.

So dance with the echoes of moments gone wild,
In the deranged laughter, we are all reconciled.
Let's twirl through the madness, no need for restraint,
For in each baffling mess, there's a grand, sweet complaint.

Curious Crossroads and Curved Paths

At the corner of laugh and tears, I stood,
Chose wrong at first, who knew I could?
Dodging a puddle, I jumped and I splashed,
Met a stranger, we both just laughed.

Sideburns and mustaches on a daring old chap,
Said, 'the best plans often take a mishap!'
Carrots in my lunch, I forgot to bring bread,
But life is a feast, with glee we're well fed.

Turning left into mayhem, right into cheer,
Every wrong turn adds flavor, I hear.
With hiccups and laughter at every bend,
Roads less traveled; they always transcend.

So here's to the journey, so curious and bright,
Where paths are all crooked, but heart's always light.
Let's skip down the lane, with joy we will stride,
In the garbled adventure, we'll take all in stride.

The Hidden Beauty of Brambles

In a garden of thorns, I found a small rose,
Abruptly I laughed at what nobody knows.
With each prick of the bramble, a chuckle arose,
In the mess of it all, a sweetness it shows.

Sunsets behind chaos, nature's own jest,
A tumble of weeds, it puts me to the test.
The rabbit I chased was just having a snack,
With giggles and snorts, I turned to the pack.

A wild crooked trail through thicket and mire,
With laughter as fuel, I'm ignited with fire.
For in tangled adventures, we find our true selves,
Like secrets of laughter tucked up on the shelves.

So here's to the brambles, thorns that surprise,
In the jumble and chaos, the beauty still lies.
Take a stroll through the wild, let your spirit roam free,
In the garden of slip-ups, there's joy, can't you see?

Fluttering Amidst the Flotsam

In a world full of scattered socks,
Dancing near the barking box,
Wanderers chase the errant breeze,
Frogs jump high with utmost ease.

Lemonade spills in the sun's warm glow,
Making sticky footprints as we go,
Fingers covered in rainbow sprinkles,
While a kite flies over wooden wrinkles.

Everything's chaos yet here we stand,
Juggling dreams with wobbly hands,
Ice-cream drips, oh what a plight,
Yet, laughter echoes through the night.

So let's twirl in this vibrant mess,
Embrace the whimsy, nothing to stress,
For in this flotsam, colors collide,
And joy, like confetti, cannot hide.

The Messy Tapestry of Being

Threadbare patterns, it's all a wreck,
Stitching smiles on a tangled trek,
Button noses with mismatched eyes,
As we dance under wobbly skies.

Peanut butter on a flying kite,
Whipped cream clouds in a noodle fight,
Tangled up in a yarn so bright,
Creating art, oh what a sight!

Scattered papers on the table lay,
Creating puzzles by night and day,
Socks that vanish, that's our trend,
But who needs order when you've got friends?

So here's to the mess we cheerfully weave,
With laughter, joy, and nothing to grieve,
In this tapestry of loony delight,
We'll make chaos our shining light.

Unfolding the Unexpected

A cake that's lopsided, icing awry,
Sprinkles tumble from clouds in the sky,
Our plans are jumble, a wild charade,
Yet every blunder is a fun escapade.

Dancing in socks on the kitchen floor,
While the cat investigates the open drawer,
Water balloons burst, laughter so loud,
We giggle together, oh, what a crowd!

Banana peels slip, oh what a ride,
With friends all around, we take it in stride,
Random moments, they twirl and tease,
Like confetti blown by a playful breeze.

So let's cheer for the quirky and strange,
In this merry mess, we can rearrange,
For the unexpected adds spice to the day,
In a wild delightful, hilarious way.

Moments of Marvelous Disorder

Juggling dishes while we eat toast,
A squirrel steals snacks—what a host!
Bubbles dancing in fizzy delight,
Turn our kitchen into sheer flight.

Wobbly chairs rock to the beat,
As mismatched socks dance on our feet,
Pancakes land with a splat and a splash,
While syrup creates a glorious mash.

Lost in readings of upside-down books,
Navigating through endless nooks,
Every misstep, an unexpected spree,
In this wonderful mess, just let it be.

For in this whirlwind, joy finds a way,
To turn every mishap into a play,
So let's keep living in delight and cheer,
In moments of disorder, do hold dear.

The Clamor of Unwritten Stories

Ink spills on pages, not all can be read,
Coffee cups witness dreams left unsaid.
Lost in a tangle of thoughts missed their chance,
Dancing to rhythms that don't have a dance.

Pages are flipped, yet silence prevails,
Characters wander through nonsensical trails.
Plot twists are hiccups, they never align,
Bantering whispers, like soup with no brine.

Jokes left on margins, a slapstick affair,
Puns trying to flee but caught in midair.
Chronicles waiting, they laugh in the wings,
While editors debate on the craziest things.

So here's to the chaos, a true writer's creed,
Drink up the blunders, for laughter's the seed.
With every mishap, a giggle will wake,
In the clamor of stories we're bound to create.

Echoes of a Shattered Compass

A compass that spins, what a curious sight,
Pointing to chaos on a starry night.
Navigating nonsense, a trip to the mall,
Finding directions, I can't find at all.

Wanderlust pulling me, round and around,
Each step leading nowhere, so lost I am bound.
Maps drawn in crayon scribble lines full of glee,
Sure, I'm going places, just not where I'd be.

The North star is laughing, the East gives a wink,
It's all quite comical – or is that what I think?
With every misstep, my heart finds its beat,
Dancing through traffic with laughable feat.

So here's to that compass, a riddle in brass,
Guiding my antics, no need to be crass.
In this shattered adventure, there's treasure to seek,
For the joy's in the journey, not just in the peak.

Daydreams in a Jumbled Reality

A toaster debates with the fridge, what a show,
Sinks planning vacations while dish soap says no.
Fairy tales pause for a breather and gasp,
While shadows of laundry engage in a clasp.

Mirrors reflect all the things left unsaid,
Whispers of socks that have fled from the bed.
Magic of nonsense, a dance on the wall,
Straight jackets of order just don't have a call.

Thoughts flit like butterflies, wildly set free,
Chasing the echoes of what's yet to be.
Reality giggles, a mad hatter's play,
With puzzles and riddles that lead us astray.

So dip into daydreams, let laughter be loud,
Join in the mayhem, a jubilant crowd.
In the jumbled reality, we paint with a grin,
Just embrace the mess, let the chaos begin!

The Symphony of Scattered Pieces

A symphony starts with a clang and a thud,
Notes tumble like marbles, all lost in the mud.
Harmonies chuckle as they trip on their tune,
Making music that howls at the light of the moon.

Instruments bicker, "You're far too off-key!"
While triangles giggle, so carefree, so free.
Drums beat in circles, a dance of dismay,
As flutes blow confetti that leads us astray.

Waltzes and jigs take a tumble, oh my!
While the bass plays tag with a wayward pie.
Strings get tangled like spaghetti on plates,
Creating a ruckus that laughter creates.

So here's to the symphony, messy and bright,
Where chaos composes the laughter of night.
In this grand orchestration of folly and cheer,
Every note just reminds us – the joy's really here!

Tangled Threads of Tomorrow

Threads are tangled, who needs a plan?
Knots in my shoelaces, just part of the jam.
Socks mismatched, shoes on the wrong feet,
Dancing through chaos, is this really a feat?

Spilled coffee stains on my bright white shirt,
Laughter erupts at my fashionable dirt.
Every mishap's a chance for a grin,
Adventure awaits; let the fun begin!

Maps are for tourists, I take the wrong street,
Finding the joy in the mess at my feet.
Dinner turned charcoal? A smoky delight,
Unplanned surprises make the evening bright!

With every distraction, delight is in store,
Life's a big joke; who could ask for more?
So here's to the chaos, the laughter, the fun,
Embracing the bumbles 'til the day is done.

Whispers in the Wind

The wind tickles me with giggles and glee,
Socks on my hands, and it's hard to see.
Chasing my shadow, where did it go?
Lost in the laughter of a friendly hello.

Trees take a bow, their leaves fly around,
I trip over roots, but I leap off the ground.
Nature's a jester with tricks up its sleeve,
In every sweet blunder, oh how I believe!

Balloons float by like silly old ghosts,
I'll chase every whim; those are the most.
Spaghetti on walls, and a cake that's too bright,
These get-togethers are pure dynamite!

Laughter like sunshine, in all that I do,
Finding treasures in moments so true.
With a heart bathed in whimsy, I'll take on the spin,
For every wild whisper, there's joy trapped within.

Chaos Under a Broken Sky

Sunshine and rain, what a magical mix,
Umbrella upside down, oh clever tricks!
Puddles for splashing and laughs that arise,
This world is a circus under wobbly skies.

I stepped in the mud with fashion in mind,
But look at the smile that I've left behind!
Spotty old shoes and a grin on my face,
It's all just a dance in this wild, silly space.

Clouds like cotton candy above my sweet head,
Giggles escape as I fall, then I tread.
While chaos may reign, I find joy in the mess,
With each little stumble, I'm feeling so blessed!

Juggling my tasks like a clown in a show,
Working through chaos; oh how I glow!
So here's to the blunders, the mess and the fun,
In a world a bit broken, I'll always outrun.

The Art of Unraveled Dreams

Tangled up wishes float down from the night,
Chasing them down; what a comical sight!
Paint splatters bright on a canvas of fate,
I'm stuck in the moment—oh, isn't it great?

Searching for meaning in socks on the floor,
Follow the trail; there may just be more.
A puzzle gone rogue, but treasure I find,
In every misstep, I'm freeing my mind.

Dancing with mishaps, we twist and we spin,
Every wrong turn reveals where I've been.
I treasure each moment, the chaos portrayed,
As I spin round and round, my heart's serenade!

So step off the path and enjoy the wild chase,
Skip all the worries; we're in this big space.
With laughter and joy, we turn voids into dreams,
The art of unravelling is bursting at seams!

Chasing Shadows in a Tangled Forest

In the woods where squirrels dance,
We trip over roots with every chance.
Chasing shadows, we lose the trail,
And giggle at our own epic fail.

Branches scratch like surprise hugs,
While leaves fall, teasing like shrugs.
We wander lost, but what a treat,
In this twisting maze, we can't be beat!

The map we drew's just a doodle,
Leading us to a wild poodle.
With each wrong turn, we redefine fun,
Laughing hard until we're done.

So let's embrace this rustling spree,
With jumbled paths and mischief, whee!
In tangled forests, we'll always find,
A comical mess, joyfully unconfined.

The Quilt of Forgotten Moments

Stitched with laughter and oddball threads,
Covering memories, where joy spreads.
Each patch a blunder, a snort or two,
Wrapped in warmth, just for me and you.

Forgotten moments all piled high,
Like socks in a dryer, oh my, oh my!
Our quilt tells stories, a mix and match,
Of coffee spills and a cheesy catch.

Doodles in the corners, hints of chaos,
There's a pizza slice and a random cat's claws.
Sipping tea spills, what a messy art,
This quilt of life, a true work of heart.

So let's cozy up under this patchwork delight,
Where every blunder turns magic at night.
In a cozy chaos, we've found our place,
A quilt of joy weaving in every space.

Joys in the Jumble

In a room full of stuff, where's my shoe?
It must be hiding with the gummy goo.
I trip on a toy, laughter erupts,
A dance with chaos, where fun interrupts.

Cookies crumbled under the table,
A snack attack gone a bit unstable.
Between the giggles and trails of crumbs,
Life's a circus, and here come the drums!

Look at the mess, but don't you fret,
Each little chaos, a joy encore set.
Finding sticks in the pockets of jeans,
Adventure lurks in the in-betweens.

So let's revel in this delightful whirl,
With jokes and laughter, give fate a twirl.
In the jumble, we stumble, but never alone,
Together we giggle, this mess feels like home.

Threads of a Chaotic Tapestry

Woven colors in a tangled spree,
Threads of chaos, wild and free.
Laughter echoes through each design,
A masterpiece of the undefined.

Where's the pattern? Who even knows?
It's just a jumble of joy that grows.
Glimmers of madness in every stitch,
Embracing the crazy, that's the pitch!

Each knot a giggle, each loop a cheer,
In this tapestry, we persevere.
Mistakes turn into delightful flair,
A quirky story, woven with care.

So let's hang it high, this brilliant mess,
A chaotic wonder, our happiness press.
In threads of laughter, we'll find our way,
Dancing through life, come what may!

Laughter in the Lunacy

In the circus of our days,
Clowns trip over their shoes.
Everyone's a jester here,
With reasons to amuse.

Juggling dreams on a tightrope,
While the audience just sighs.
Every fall's a funny twist,
With laughter in our eyes.

Embracing the Beautiful Chaos

Colors splash like paintballs,
In a gallery of glee.
Each mistake a brushstroke,
On this canvas wild and free.

Mismatched socks on parade,
Oh, what an artful sight!
Stumbling into embraces,
In the chaos, we take flight.

A Symphony of Missteps

Banging pots in the kitchen,
As the cat tries to dance.
Each note a wild surprise,
Like fate's quirky romance.

The maestro drops the baton,
And the band just goes rogue.
Unexpected harmonies,
In a glorious wallow.

Navigating the Unknown

Maps are written in crayon,
With arrows pointing south.
We sail on paper boats,
Winding through each mouth.

Every misdirection's laughter,
As we drift on silly tides.
Adventure is a bumpy ride,
With giggles as our guides.

Scribbled Signs on a Winding Road

A sign that says, 'Turn Right at Chaos,'
And then it points directly to a cactus.
Follow the arrows, oh what a panic,
   Is that a road or a game of manic?

Round every corner, a cow in a tutu,
Dancing to music played by a shoe.
Just when you think it's all going fine,
   You trip on a sock, you trip on a vine.

The map's a mess, it's like modern art,
   Crayons scribbed, it fell apart.
But stumbling is fun, don't you agree?
   Grab a balloon, let's float with glee!

So, onward we go with a laugh and a cheer,
   Life's crazy dance has nothing to fear.
With each twist and turn, a brand new jest,
   In this winding road, we're truly blessed.

Twirls in the Turbulence

The world spins like a dervish at dawn,
Spilling my coffee, oh what a con!
Grab your hats, it's a windy affair,
Can't find my shoes? Who needs a pair?

Up in the air, a sandwich takes flight,
Flies to the sun, oh what a sight!
Join the circus of socks and rhymes,
Life's a jigsaw, lost in the chimes.

Spinning through chaos, I'm dizzy and bold,
Every blunder's a story to be told.
Just catch the laughter, let's make a pact,
In the whirlwind of fun, there's no need to act.

So twirl with me, in this beautiful mess,
With giggles and grins, we are truly blessed.
Wrap up your worries, toss them away,
In this dance of mishaps, let's seize the day!

Whirlwinds of Wonder

A cat on a skateboard zooms past my door,
Chasing a squirrel that's never a bore.
Flamingos in bowties, oh what a sight,
Who needs to reason? It feels so right.

My thoughts are lost, tripping on dreams,
Finding new flavors in cherry ice creams.
The laundry's a mountain, the dishes a beast,
Yet together we laugh, let's feast like a feast.

Twirls of confusion, they dance in my head,
With giggles and snorts, I'd rather be led.
Life's not a burden, it's more like a jest,
In the whirlwinds of wonder, we're truly blessed.

Every mishap is magic, a spark in the night,
Embracing the chaos feels oh so right.
So here's to the whirlwinds and backflips of fate,
Join in the laughter, don't hesitate!

The Untamed Symphony of Experience

A symphony of hiccups begins to play,
With one broken drum and a cat's ballet.
Trombones are squeaking, and trumpets are bent,
Yet the laughter it brings? Oh, it's heaven sent.

Meet the maestro, a fish in the bowl,
Conducting the chaos with one little roll.
Strings of spaghetti, they dance with such flair,
In the untamed orchestra, we all share.

The audience chuckles at every mistake,
As a trumpet toots loudly, causing a quake.
Misfit instruments join in the fun,
In this raucous concert, we're all number one.

So let's raise our glasses to this wild jam,
Lost in the rhythm, who gives a damn?
In the symphony's chaos, with laughter we blend,
With every odd note, we joyously mend.

Embracing the Entropy

In mismatched socks we wander,
With cereal stuck in hair,
We laugh at all our blunders,
And dance without a care.

The coffee spills, the dishes pile,
The cat just stole my chair,
We wear our chaos like a style,
And breathe in messy air.

Chasing whims like wild kites,
With strings all tangled tight,
We trip on our own silly nights,
And still, we feel just right.

A glorious jumble, a joyful mess,
In the chaos, we find bliss,
We'll toast to laughter, love, and stress,
In this whirlwind, we persist.

Kaleidoscope of Confusion

My plans are like a jigsaw,
With pieces lost in time,
A game of hide and seek,
A punchline with no rhyme.

The GPS is feeling bold,
It leads me into trees,
But every wrong turn's a story told,
A trip full of unease.

Our schedules go on holiday,
They've left me feeling giddy,
We'll make bread, it's half past May,
And witness the city's pity.

In swirling hues, we twirl and spin,
Confusion's our best friend,
So let the muddle start again,
With laughter as our trend.

Whispers in the Wilderness

Out in the woods, I sought some peace,
   But squirrels had other plans,
  They've made my hat a cozy feast,
    My picnic's in their hands.

The trail's a loop, I'm back again,
   A compass lost in haze,
  But I just grin at the absurd,
    And wander in a daze.

The leaves conspire with the breeze,
   They tickle me with glee,
A walk that feels like pure unease,
    But that's just fine with me.

In nature's heart, we laugh and stray,
   Each twist a joy to find,
  Embracing chaos every day,
    In whispers soft and kind.

Tangles of Tomorrow

My to-do list's quite a pickle,
It wrestles with my will,
But every knot is just a trickle,
Of laughter, free and shrill.

Plans rise like soufflés, then they flop,
I juggle them all day,
Yet each mishap makes me hop,
And laugh my stress away.

The calendar's a snapshot,
Of moments gone astray,
But oh, the joy can't be forgot,
In tangles of the play.

So here's to bliss in every twist,
A hearty cheer, hooray!
For in the mess, that's where the gist,
Of fun and dreams convey.

In the Midst of Disorder

A sock is hiding, quite the thief,
My keys have vanished, oh what a grief!
Pants inside out, they dance with glee,
In this crazy maze, just let me be.

Breakfast spills like a wild parade,
Cereal swimming in lemonade.
My coffee's gone cold, a sad little fate,
Yet laughter erupts; isn't chaos great?

The cat's on the table, the dog's in my chair,
I step on a Lego, oh the pain I bear!
Yet in all this madness, I find a smile,
Jumbling through life, it's my favorite style.

So toast to the mess, let's aim for a cheer,
For every small hiccup that brings us near.
Here's to the tangles, the chaos and fun,
In this wild ride, we're all number one!

Finding Beauty in the Fray

A pizza slice meets an old shoe lace,
Spaghetti dances, a pasta embrace.
My plants think they're on a rollercoaster,
They thrive on chaos, a leafy mobster.

A jigsaw puzzle with missing parts,
Each piece a memory, some break our hearts.
Crumbs of joy scattered all around,
Finding gems where the chaos is found.

The cat naps on papers, the dog sends a bark,
Neighbors peek in, wondering 'What's that spark?'
Yet here in the mayhem, I find my flair,
Messy moments, oh how they declare!

In spills and thrills, there's beauty we chase,
With every mishap, a joyful embrace.
So let's waltz through the clutter, arms open wide,
In this fray of life, let's take it in stride!

Unplugged Melodies in a Noisy World

There's music in chaos, a symphony loud,
As toys sing their songs, a joyous crowd.
Dishwashers hum while the children play,
In this wild orchestra, I'd love to stay.

A blender whirs as the dog starts to bark,
The clock ticks in concert, putting joy in the dark.
Neighbors drum with laughter, the door creaks just right,
In this cacophony, everything's bright.

The vacuum's a monster, chasing away dust,
As socks get lost in a footwear bust.
Yet in these strange sounds, a tune unfolds,
Melodies of madness, a harmony bold.

Sometimes I wish for a moment of hush,
But then I remember the joy in the rush.
So let's raise our voices to the rhythm we found,
In this jumbled concert, let happiness astound!

Unscripted Scenes of Tomorrow

The script is lost, like my right shoe,
I tripped on a moment, world spun askew.
Yesterday's plans, they tangled and twirled,
In this unscripted show, I'm ready to twirl.

Actors are giggling, lines thrown away,
A fish in a tutu steals the day.
With no cue cards, we dance to our fate,
In this messy play, it's never too late.

The scene keeps changing, plot lines collide,
I'll wear mismatched socks with unbridled pride.
With silly defeats and sweet little wins,
In this laugh-out-loud drama, we all wear grins.

So here's to the moments unplanned and weird,
For every slip-up, a chuckle is cheered.
We'll scribble our journey, let spontaneity flow,
In this grand comedy, let's steal the show!

The Road Less Traveled by Messy Feet

With shoes all caked in mud, oh what a sight,
Each step a little slip, but it feels so right.
Paths unplanned, oh where will they lead?
Every corner a giggle, every turn a stampede.

Laughter dances with dirt on my toes,
Stumbling through chaos, oh how it grows.
No map in hand, just a heart that's free,
Why take the straight road when you can be me?

Footprints tell stories no one can trace,
Wipe that frown off, let's quicken the pace.
Sloshing in puddles, our journey is grand,
With messy feet, together we stand.

Stories Inscribed in the Mud.

A squelch and a splash greet the morning call,
Each muddy mishap, we giggle and sprawl.
Footprints like secrets, they whisper and sway,
In this messy old world, we'll find our own way.

With splatters of brown on our pants and our shoes,
We chart our own course, we've nothing to lose.
Each stumble and slip just adds to the flair,
In the tapestry of mud, freedom's laid bare.

A canvas of chaos, of laughter and fun,
In each muddy corner, our stories are spun.
So let's dive right in, let's embrace the mess,
For it's here in the muddle that we're truly blessed.

Fragments of Chaos

Scattered bits of glitter and crumpled dreams,
The universe chuckles, or so it seems.
Jumbled puzzles, what a crazy array,
Who needs a neat plan? Let's just play!

Chaos twirls in a vibrant ballet,
With mismatched socks leading the way.
Each odd little moment a treasure to save,
In the mess of existence, we dance and we rave.

Pieces of laughter, with crumbs on the floor,
In the chaos we find what we truly adore.
So let's raise a glass to this topsy-turvy ride,
With fragments of madness, let joy be our guide.

The Art of Unraveled Threads

A tangle of yarn spun without any care,
Knots like our dreams caught up in mid-air.
Stitch by stitch, the fabric unfolds,
In the chaos we craft a story untold.

We're weaving a blanket of laughter and fun,
Pausing for snacks, then we're back on the run.
With threads all askew, we embrace the mishap,
In the mess of creation, we find our own map.

So let's color outside every line that we trace,
With hearts wide open, we'll pick up the pace.
In the art of unravelling, we discover it's true,
The beauty is messy, just like me and you.

The Secrets of a Tangled Journey

Stumbling over socks and shoes,
Tripping on the daily blues.
Coffee spills on the morning toast,
Chasing the paper that I lost.

Maps are crumpled, plans go awry,
Cats chase shadows, oh my, oh my!
The cereal never quite hits the bowl,
Every day's a new, zany stroll.

Laughter echoes in crowded rooms,
While chaos dances, here comes the boom!
Moments of joy in a tangle of threads,
Dancing on tables, so far from my bed.

We're all just puzzles missing a piece,
In this wacky ride, let's find our release.
With each twist and turn, we'll make a stand,
Embracing the mess, hand in hand.

Cacophony of Unexpected Notes

A trumpet blares out of tune,
While kitchen clocks tick to a cartoon.
The cat conducts a symphony loud,
As dad attempts to sing, proud.

Dishes stack like a leaning tower,
Plant pots sprout in the daily shower.
Lost in a shuffle, socks go flying,
In this chaos, no point in crying.

The phone rings twice, but no one's there,
While I search for a matching pair.
We joke and laugh at the sweet disarray,
Finding joy in the fray of the day.

Balloons float off into the sky,
As we wave goodbye with a sigh.
In the whimsical chaos, we find grace,
In the messiness, there's a happy place.

Radiance in the Fractured

Cracks in the mug, but it holds tea,
A toaster that talks back to me.
Sticky notes wait on the fridge like stars,
As life throws lemons adorned with scars.

Socks don't match, but who even cares?
With mismatched patterns, we're true dare bears.
A dance of coffee spills and crumbs,
In the laughter and chaos, happiness hums.

Wobbly tables and chairs askew,
But laughter gives it a vibrant hue.
Here's to the moments that don't quite align,
In this fractured radiance, we'll be just fine.

Every mishap's an artful twist,
Lessons learned in a quirky mist.
So let's toast to the oddball cheer,
In this tangle of mess, let's shift into gear.

Elements of a Beautiful Disaster

Dried spaghetti on the kitchen floor,
A heaping mountain of laundry galore.
Spilled juice stains on the little town map,
Finding treasures in a happy mishap.

Surprises lurk in the back of the fridge,
While goldfish leap like they're at a bridge.
We dance in circles, full of delight,
Finding rhythm in the silly plight.

A custard pie lands right on my nose,
As laughter erupts in spirited throes.
With every blunder, let's make a toast,
To beautiful chaos, we love the most.

So here's to the mess, the wild and absurd,
In this whirl of madness, joy is stirred.
Embrace the chaos, don't let it pass,
For in every disaster, beauty is mass.

Wading Through the Wilderness

In the woods, I trudge ahead,
With tangled vines around my head.
A squirrel laughs, I trip and fall,
My sense of direction? Not at all.

Trees are talking, though I doubt,
They whisper secrets, jest, and shout.
I wave to birds who mock my gait,
Why did I think this was first-rate?

Out of the bushes, a deer pops out,
He winks and snickers, oh stinky route!
Nature's charm, a baffling mess,
With every step, I must confess.

Yet in this jungle, wide and vast,
I find the giggles that hold me fast.
Through muddled paths and silly trails,
I grin at life, for laughter prevails.

Emotions Like Flickering Lights

My heart's a lamp, it flickers bright,
One minute joyful, then scared of height.
It flashes red, then dims to blue,
Oh, what's a feeling? I haven't a clue!

Like disco balls in a cramped hall,
Shiny and bouncing, then fade, then call.
Giddy with glee, then down in the dumps,
I ride this wave of giggles and grumps.

Baking muffins, I'm ready to cheer,
But end up with batter stuck in my ear.
Oh emotions, a slapstick play,
With scenes that change from night to day.

Yet through this show, I find a spark,
In every quirk, there's joy to mark.
Through ups and downs, I'll dance along,
For in this chaos, we all belong.

The Chaotic Dance of Shadows

Shadows waltz across my floor,
They trip and stumble, can't find the door.
In a jitterbug, they twist and twirl,
One shadow's wearing a colorful swirl.

A conga line breaks into a mess,
With every bump, they lose their dress.
They giggle and pout, oh what a sight,
Dance parties happen deep in the night.

Laughter echoes, a bright parade,
In the corner, the shadows mislaid.
They play tag with the moon's soft grin,
Two-stepping wild, let the fun begin!

And as they dance, I join their play,
Spinning in circles, we sway away.
In this wild rumba, we're all just friends,
In the chaos of shadows, the laughter never ends.

A Serenade of Uncertainty

Strumming chords on a guitar so wild,
The notes are messy but life's a child.
Do I play fast, or slow the pace?
The song gets lost in this chaotic space.

"I need a rhyme!" my brain declares,
But laughter bubbles, it just doesn't care.
Dance with the rhythm, who knows the key?
It's just a tune, let it be free!

Melodies mix like a salad bowl,
Tossed with surprises, that's the goal!
A dash of giggles, a sprinkle of fun,
In this serenade, we're all just one.

So here's to the notes that wander astray,
To the quirks we embrace, come what may.
For in this tune of sweet uncertainty,
Lies the magic of a jumbled journey.

www.ingramcontent.com/pod-product-compliance
Lightning Source LLC
Chambersburg PA
CBHW051631160426
43209CB00004B/605